I0166787

KIDDING GOATS

A SIMPLE GUIDE

FELICITY MCCULLOUGH

Paperback Edition

ISBN: 978-1-78165-053-0

Series: Goat Knowledge 13

My Lap Shop Publishers
Plymouth, England
www.mylapshop.com

Table Of Contents

Disclaimer

This book is meant to be STRICTLY AN EDUCATIONAL AND INFORMATIONAL TOOL ONLY.

The suggestions contained in this material might not be suitable for everyone. It is not intended to provide diagnosis or treatment.

The author obtained the information from sources believed to be reliable and from personal experience. Although the best effort was made by the author, there are no guarantees as to the accuracy or completeness of the contents within this work.

The author does not guarantee the accuracy of any information or content in resources or websites listed or cited within this work.

Additionally, the author, publisher and distributors never give medical, legal, accounting or any other type of professional advice. The reader must always seek those services from competent professionals that can review the particular circumstances. Mention of any product, brand or website is NOT an endorsement or recommendation of that product, service or usage.

The medical field is a very dynamic field that is constantly undergoing research, modifications and advancements and therefore information contained in this book should always be researched further and A VETERINARIAN OR OTHER SPECIALIST SHOULD BE CONSULTED where appropriate.

Any and all application of the information contained in this book is of the sole responsibility of the person performing said action. The author, publisher and distributors particularly disclaim any liability, loss, or risk taken by individuals who directly or indirectly act on the information herein. All readers must accept full responsibility for their use of this material.

Publishers

My Lap Shop Publishers

91 Mayflower Street, Unit 222,

Plymouth, Devon, PL1 1SB

Kidding Or Parturition

Kidding or parturition is the act or process of giving birth. Generally speaking, does have little trouble kidding. They usually need little human interference. In fact, many does actually prefer to be alone at this time. All you, the producer, has to do is check in every once in a while to make sure that things are progressing normally.

In order for you to know that things are progressing normally, you need to understand the kidding process.

Length Of Gestation

Goat gestation or pregnancy lasts from 142 to 157 days. The average is roughly 147 to 150 days, or five months. The length of the gestation can vary. Sometimes the gestation is longer or shorter.

Longer gestation periods can be caused by late-maturing breeds. Male offspring results in longer gestations as well. Single births and heavier offspring are other factors which prolong the gestation period. Gestation can be shorter with female offspring, multiple births, lighter offspring, and prolific, or meat goat breeds.

Planning The Due Date And Keeping Records

The producer can figure out roughly when the babies are due. This is where record keeping plays such an important role. It's a question of simple arithmetic if you record the breeding date.

It is important to have at least a rough estimate of the due date, so that you will be prepared and ready for babies. Knowing the due date is also important so that you can plan the doe's management, including when to vaccinate and de-worm and to make sure she gets the proper nutrition at the appropriate time.

You will also know when you should crutch the does with long hair. Crutching is a practice where the hairs around the vulva, backside and teats are clipped. The practice is done to facilitate cleaning after kidding and also to make sure that the kids will be able to find the teats without a problem.

The breeding date is not the only piece of information that you can keep. The more detailed the records, the more information you will have at your fingertips. More information can help you plan for the future, or figure out why something went wrong.

Writing down any observations, the date that the male was introduced and removed, as well as any accidental exposures are all interesting information to note down.

Kidding Supplies

The **Phone number** of your veterinarian in case of emergencies or questions.

Iodine Tincture (7%) to dip the kids' navel cords

Plastic container to put the iodine in. Plastic film canisters or cow teat cups are best.

Sterile fish line or **dental floss** to tie off the kid's navel cords if necessary.

Towels or **rags** that are kept clean and dry. These are used to dry kids off if necessary.

Soap or **disinfectant scrub** used to clean hands and arms and the doe when a procedure is about to be done.

Thermometer

Plastic sleeves or **gloves** to be used when performing internal examinations, or when handling placentas, or aborted foetuses.

Lubricant

Hot water

Collar and Lead Rope used to restrain the doe.

Baby Basal Syringe, or Basting Syringe used to clear the baby's mouth and nose.

Flashlight

Head Snare/Baby Puller

Listening Device such as a baby monitor, walkie talkie, or cell phone.

Antiseptic solutions such as Nolvasan or Betadine to disinfect equipment and skin.

Antibiotics such as Procaine Penicillin G. Make sure to consult a veterinarian before administering, to make sure that dosages are correct and to know about withdrawal periods.

Propylene Glycol and **50% Dextrose, or Glucose** is energy for goats that need it.

Calcium Gluconate

Tubing and **Syringe (60 cc)** for tube feeding **weak kids.**

Colostrum – frozen colostrum, or colostrum substitute.

Heating supplies to heat up hypothermic kids. Such supplies include a warming box, heating pad, or blow dryer.

Bottle for bottle feeding orphans. A 10 to 16-ounce soda bottle with nipple works well.

Baking soda is needed to treat acidosis and Floppy Kid Syndrome.

Electrolytes are important for dehydrated kids.

Recording materials can range from good old-fashioned paper and pencil, to computerized systems.

CD & T Vaccines

BoSe injections if you are in an area that is deficient in Selenium.

Syringes and **needles** as needed for injecting both kids and adults.

Eartagger and **tags** for permanent identification.

Scale to weigh animals accurately for dosages and records.

De-worming Medication.

Kidding Location

Does should be moved to the location where you want them to give birth about a month before the due date. Doing this allows enough time for the doe to get accustomed and comfortable to the new location.

It is best to kid indoors, because kids are more likely to survive. The area should have bedding and be draught-free. Kidding outdoors is not impossible though, as long as the pasture, or area is clean and the weather is warm enough.

The area should have a jug. A jug is a separate location where the doe and her kids are placed for one to three days to help with the bonding process. Separating them from the rest of the herd also facilitates management and makes sure that other females can't "steal" the babies.

Signs Of Approaching Parturition

As the time of birth gets near, you can keep an eye out for some changes, which occurs in the doe. These changes will let you know roughly how close you are to the birth. Knowing this can make all of the difference in the unlikely case that something should go wrong.

The following are things that you should take into consideration. Keep in mind, though that each doe is an individual and there is no set pattern that *every* doe will demonstrate in a set order. The only time you will be 100% sure that the birth is eminent is when it actually occurs.

The doe's behaviour will change. Goats are herd animals and prefer to be with their herd, yet as birthing approaches, the doe will separate from the herd, isolating herself. She will act more territorial, restless and nervous, as evidenced by her inability to sit still. She will constantly get up and lay down. Her tail will twitch and she will urinate frequently. She will paw at the ground, which indicates abdominal pain. She will also display a reduced appetite on the day of the kidding.

Physical changes will accompany the behavioural changes. The udder will fill up and become firm, which is the one of the biggest indicators that birth is eminent. The teats will become engorged and there will be vaginal discharge. The muscles in the hip will become relaxed and the belly will drop, while the sides cave in. The vulva will also become swollen.

Stages Of Parturition

There are three stages of parturition: (1) Preparation, (2) Expulsion and (3) Cleaning or After Birth.

Stage 1 - Preparation

Stage one of parturition is the Preparation Stage. It usually lasts around 12 to 24 hours and is characterized by rhythmic contractions, cervix dilation, foetus positioning, and mucous discharge. The most important part of this stage is cervix dilation. The widest part of the foetus is the hips. So, the passing of the hips can be considered as the hardest part of the delivery.

The normal position of the foetus is in a "dive" position where the head is resting on the forelegs, which are extended in front of the foetus. The soles of the hooves are resting downwards.

Another position that is usually considered normal is backwards, although this position is not as desirable as the dive position, since it is best if the head comes out first. Having the head coming out fast ensures that it is more likely that the baby breathes air, instead of aspirating birthing fluids. All other presentations are considered as problematic.

Stage 2 - Expulsion

Stage two is the expulsion stage, where the foetus leaves the mother's body and is welcomed into the world. The doe may remain standing, or may lie down for this stage. Some does want to be left alone at this stage, while others prefer company.

The stage begins when the water bag ruptures. The baby should be born forty-five to sixty minutes after the water sac breaks, or thirty to thirty-five minutes after the front legs are visible. Babies in a multiple birth should be born within 30 minutes of each other.

The doe should not forcefully strain for much longer than sixty minutes. If she is still straining, then you should either try to assist the birth or get help from another more experienced producer, or a veterinarian.

Stage 3 – Cleaning

The third stage is the last stage. This is the cleaning stage, or after birth. Roughly thirty to sixty minutes after the birth of the last baby, the placenta or afterbirth is expelled. The uterus will return to almost its normal size and shape. Full involution normally takes more than a month.

The placenta is a red, liver-like mass with strawberry-like lumps and whitish cords. Normally, does will eat the placenta. This is an instinct that comes from the wild, where it could attract predators. The placenta contains the hormone oxytocin. Oxytocin helps with milk let down and uterine involution.

It is best not to permit the doe to eat the placenta, though, because there are diseases that are transmitted via infected placenta, like Scrapie and some other abortive diseases. Another reason is that the placenta is very indigestible.

You are going to have to do something with it, though. You can't just leave it, because you don't want to attract wild animals, predators and scavengers. You shouldn't let the guard dogs eat it either, although many people do permit it.

Assisting With Deliveries

There are times when you feel that the doe needs to be assisted in delivering her babies. The key to assisting with deliveries is to be clean, gentle, calm and patient.

The first step is to catch and confine the doe. The doe can then be laid down on her back, or hoisted up depending on the problem.

Next, clean the doe's vulva area. Then remove any watch, rings or other jewellery from the hands and arms and make sure that your nails are short. Wash your hands and arms.

Either dry your hands on a clean cloth or let them air dry, making sure not to touch anything. Put on gloves or OB sleeves when your hands or dry. Lubricate the gloves with plenty of lubricant. Good lubricants include lubricant jelly, obstetrical lubricant, bland soap and water, or even shortening. Just make sure that there is plenty of it on the gloves and in the vagina.

Make a triangle with your fingers by touching your fingers to your thumb. Insert your hand in the doe's vagina GENTLY. Always be as gentle as possible, to avoid injuring the doe or stressing her out more.

When inside, try to determine the position of the baby. Correct if necessary. When the baby is in place, cup the hooves in your hand to ensure that they don't damage the doe's uterus and apply traction. If progress isn't accomplished in 30 minutes, call a veterinarian, or someone with more experience.

Administer antibiotics such as LA-200 in does if there were any problems with the birth, especially if you had to go in pretty far. The best option is injectable antibiotics, because they are act faster and have more prolonged action. There are certain antibiotics that can be poured inside depending on the problem.

What To Do With The Babies

If there was a problem with the birth or the kids had problems, you may need to revive the baby. The first step is to clear the mucous from the airway. There are a few ways that the airways can be cleared:

You can insert a piece of straw or hay into the baby's nose. Move it around, gently tickling the skin. This will make the baby sneeze, which clears the airway.

Raising the front legs expands the chest cavity and can help breathing.

Some people hang the baby by the hind legs and swing it in a circle. Make sure that you have a good grip and that you don't lose the baby. If the baby slips from your grasp, it could hit a wall, ceiling, or floor resulting in serious injury, or even death.

Blow air into lungs. Hold the mouth shut and blow in the nose. Not everyone is comfortable with this option.

When the baby is breathing, place it in front of the doe's nose. She will hopefully take over from there and will clean and warm the baby.

If she doesn't, use towels to do the job for her. Drying and warming the baby is important to prevent hypothermia, one of the leading causes of death in kids.

The doe and the babies should be put into the jug together. This is a small pen where the animals will be kept for one to three days, to facilitate management and to help the bonding process.

Clip the navel cord if it is longer than three or four inches from the kid's belly. Disinfect the navel cords with Betadine, or Iodine in a plastic container. Camera film canisters or cow teat dipping cups are excellent for this.

Squeeze out a tiny bit of colostrum from each teat. This is called stripping the teat. A wax plug forms on the end of the teat, which seals the teat from the outside world. This is to prevent bacteria from getting in. Squeezing out a bit of milk also checks the milk supply, making sure that there is food for the baby.

One of the most important things for the producer to do is to observe the baby and make sure that it drinks. The first milk produced is called colostrum and is vital to the kid's health, because it is full of nutrition and antibodies. Antibodies are produced by the doe and will protect the baby from disease for roughly a month or so, until the baby's own immune system is mature enough to take over

Things That Can Go Wrong

Sometimes, though, things can go wrong with a kidding. In this section, we'll cover some of the more common problems that can crop up, how to recognize the problem and what to do about them.

Pregnancy Toxaemia

Pregnancy Toxaemia can be called by a few other names, including Sleeping Sickness, Ketosis, Lambing Paralysis, and Twin Lamb Disease. Pregnancy Toxaemia is characterised by low blood glucose, caused by insufficient intake of energy during late pregnancy. If the doe doesn't get enough to eat, she will automatically break down fat into toxic ketone bodies.

Does that are most susceptible to getting this problem are females carrying multiple foetuses, obese females, thin females, old females and timid females.

Pregnancy Toxaemia is most likely to occur during the final trimester of pregnancy. The doe that is experiencing this disease will lag behind the others and be depressed. They will also exhibit neurological symptoms, such as walking unsteady, salivation, splayed out rear legs, lack of appetite, lying down unable to get up. The disease can be fatal.

Treatment consists of intravenously administering oral Propylene Glycol, Dextrose, Calcium Borogluconate, and vitamin B-complex. If the situation is more severe, the foetus should also be removed either by inducing parturition, or caesarean section.

Milk Fever

Milk Fever is also known as Hypocalcaemia, meaning low blood calcium. This disease occurs during late pregnancy or early lactation, especially with dairy goats. It is characterised by low blood calcium.

Females with this disease will show symptoms similar to Pregnancy Toxaemia. The treatment is simply supplying calcium. The calcium can be administered orally, subcutaneously, or intravenously.

Abortion

Abortion is the early termination of pregnancy. Abortion can be caused by many things including toxins, trauma, unviable offspring, stress and disease. Diseases that can cause abortions include Chlamydia, Campylobacter, Toxoplasmosis and Salmonella.

Producers can tell that an abortion has occurred by the presence of stillborn babies, foetuses, weak, or premature babies. Females may be sick for several days before she aborts late in her pregnancy, or not.

Some abortions are normal. Notice above that one of the potential reasons that a doe can abort, is the presence of unviable offspring. Abortion can be a necessary part of life. The problem comes when there are too many abortions.

One major problem can arise from an Abortion Storm. An abortion storm is when many abortions happen to most, if not all of the females in the herd. This is normally caused by something contagious like a virus, or bacteria.

When a contagion enters the herd for the first time, it can cause an abortion storm once and only once.

After that only new animals or young animals will experience an abortion in their first gestations. Normally after the one abortion, the female develops immunity and no longer aborts.

Abortions are controlled by isolating the aborting does and properly disposing of foetuses, the placenta and fluids. This is extremely important, because a contaminated pasture can remain contaminated for a long time. The females should be injected with antibiotics, including the females that didn't abort.

It is best if every effort is made to find the cause of the abortion. To do this, you will need to work with a diagnostic veterinarian and veterinary laboratories. The vet will collect samples from the aborted foetuses and materials to send to the lab.

Prevent abortions by feeding or injecting antibiotics and vaccinating against the diseases that cause abortions. Controlling the cat population prevents the spread of Toxoplasmosis because cats are major transmitters of the microorganism, especially kittens. Adult cats are less likely to transmit the disease.

Vaginal Prolapse

Vaginal Prolapse is when the tissue of the vagina is pushed out of the body. It happens most commonly during the last month of pregnancy. It is not as common in goats as in other species, yet it can still occur.

Factors which can predispose vaginal prolapse and possible causes include the presence of multiple foetuses and increased rumen fill due to poor quality forage such as phytoestrogenic forages.

Phytoestrogenic means that a plant contains a substance that acts similar to the hormone oestrogen.

Gravity, overcrowding, lack of exercise, obesity with a lot of intra-abdominal fat and genetic predisposition are other factors and potential causes. Obesity, previous history and genetics are the most important factors.

Vaginal prolapse is an extremely painful condition and the doe will need to be treated with pain relief first. Clean the vagina and surrounding area with mild soapy water. Then, replace the vagina within the doe's body.

If it occurs once, there is a 40% chance of it occurring again. There are a few options used to keep the vagina in and prevent another occurrence. These options include a spoon or bearing retainer, prolapse harness, prolapse truss, and purse-string suture. If the suture is used, remember to remove the suture before kidding.

The problem usually corrects itself after kidding, though both the doe and her offspring should be culled.

Dystocia

Dystocia is simply defined as a difficult birth. There are practically countless reasons why this can happen. Some of the more common causes of dystocia are the wrong positioning of the foetus, the failure of the cervix to dilate or incomplete dilation, the presence of a baby that is too large for the doe, and vaginal prolapse.

Some contributing factors include a young or old doe, obesity, oversized foetuses resulting from over-feeding the doe in late gestation, small pelvic area, certain breeds, males that sire big babies, lack of exercise and multiple births.

To correct babies that are in the wrong position, push the kid slightly back into womb, cup hoof in your palm, extending the legs.

Cupping the hooves will prevent them from hurting the mother's uterus. If the head is out, wash the head before putting back inside the female.

Positions that are easy to correct: elbow lock, one leg back, both legs back and swollen head. Positions that are harder to correct include tight birth, head back, breech and simultaneous.

A tight birth is when the mom is too small and or the baby is too big for whatever reason. Use a lot of lubricant and firm pressure.

Pull skin over the kid's head, extend legs one at a time.

Head back is self-explanatory position. Push the baby back and then turn the head.

Breech is when the baby is backwards. Cut the fetlocks and extend the rear legs forward. This is one of the positions where it is very important to deliver quickly, so that the baby's first breath is out of the womb and it doesn't inhale fluids.

A simultaneous malposition is when you have more than one

foetus trying to come out at the same time. The hardest part of this birth is that you have to figure out and separate the foetuses.

Certain problems are extremely unpleasant to deal with. These include dead, deformed and decomposed babies. You should consider getting a veterinarian, or another more experienced goat herder involved. if you've never dealt with these problems before.

Ringwomb

Ringwomb is the name of the condition where there is a complete or partial failure of cervix dilation. We don't really understand what causes it. Some theories include abortion, premature birth and genetics of foetus.

Partial dilation is treated by manually stimulating the cervix, or using the drug Oxytocin. If it is complete or "true" Ringwomb then a Caesarean section is needed to remove the baby, because nothing will work to open the cervix. Does with Ringwomb should be culled.

Retained Placenta

A Retained Placenta is the failure to expel placenta, or afterbirth after twelve to eighteen hours. Gently tug the placenta to see if it detaches. Do not forcibly pull it out. You may need to get a veterinarian involved.

Causes and contributing factors to retained placentas include abortion, stillbirths, premature birth, uterine infection, difficult or prolonged birth, assisted delivery, dead baby still in uterus, nutritional deficiencies, exhaustion and or stress.

Sometimes the doe lacks calcium, which is important for muscular contractions. Without adequate levels of calcium, the doe is unable to expel the uterus. Administering Calcium Borogluconate will give an added boost, just in case the doe needs it.

Oxytocin and prostaglandin are drugs, which will stimulate uterine contractions. These are administered to see if the doe can manage to expel the placenta on her own. Antibiotics are also administered to prevent uterine infection.

Uterine Prolapse

The uterus is turned inside out in this disorder and pushed through the birth canal. You see a mass coming out of the doe's vagina. It can happen right after kidding, or a few days later. It is life threatening and needs to be treated like an emergency. Call your veterinarian.

Causes and predisposing factors include uterine infection, retained placenta, difficult or prolonged birth, nutritional deficiencies, obesity and genetics.

First protect the uterus by wrapping it in a plastic bag and or clean cloths. The doe will require an epidural, which is local anaesthetics or Lidocaine, applied into the base of the spinal cord, just above the tail.

Next, the uterus can be cleansed with a solution of water and sugar. The sugar may reduce swelling. Elevate the animal's hindquarters and replace the uterus. Pouring five gallons of water into the replaced uterus will help weigh it down within the body and prevent it from being expelled again. A purse string suture is used as well. Finally, Oxytocin, Calcium Borogluconate and systemic antibiotics should be administered.

Agalactia

Agalactia is a condition where the doe does not give milk, or there is a delayed milk let down. Causes can be hormonal, nutritional, difficult birthing, stress, and such diseases as mastitis, or CAE.

Treat Agalactia with Oxytocin. Oxytocin not only stimulates uterine contractions, it also works on the glands that produce the milk. You may need to tube feed babies colostrum, cross foster them, or bottle-feed them until the milk comes.

Rejection

Sometimes a doe will reject one or more of her babies.

Rejection happens with new or high-strung mothers, or when the mother over-bonded with the first baby.

Rejection can also happen if the second baby has a slow arrival, when the babies are separated from the mother, when the mother has painful or sensitive udder, painful teats, or the baby has sharp teeth.

Other potential rejection reasons, include babies that got swapped, abandonment, the doe can't tell how many babies she has and racism. It's true, goats are racist. If a doe has a baby with different coloured hair, she may reject it.

Possible solutions to this problem is to put the dam in a

jug, or pen with her babies, put the baby in front of the dam's nose, try to fool dam with different odours, manually hold the dam for nursing, put the dam in a head stanchion, rear the babies artificially, or give away the babies.

Resources

Schoenian, Susan. Parturition. 2011 Ewe and Doe Management Webinar Series. Available at https://connect.moo.umd.edu/p9 9147177/?launcher=false&fcsCo ntent=true&pbMode=normal.

McCullough, Felicity. Success Guide for Raising Healthy Goats. CreateSpace. 2012.

Cornell University Cooperative Extension. Kidding with Confidence: A Kidding Season Mentoring Program for Northeast Meat Goat Producers. 2008.

Available at: -
http://www.ansci.cornell.edu/goat
s/Resources/GoatArticles/GoatH
ealth/KidCare/KiddingHandbook.
pdf.

My Lap Shop Publishers, 91
Mayflower Street, Unit 222,
Plymouth, Devon PL1 1SB UK

Acknowledgements

The publisher thanks Danielle Shurskis for her support and help in bringing these series of books to publication.

Cover Photograph

Diane Doiron ©

Magnificent Hill.ca

http://magnificenthill.wordpress.com/

Publishers

My Lap Shop Publishers

91 Mayflower Street, Unit 222,

Plymouth, Devon, PL1 1SB

United Kingdom

Tel: +44 (0)871 560 5297

www.mylapshop.com

www.goatlapshop.com

About My Lap Shop Publishers

First Edition September 2012

ISBN - 978-1-78165-053-0

About Felicity McCullough

Felicity McCullough has written several books about preventative health care for goats.

The website dedicated to goats www.goatlapshop.com has a wide variety of topics and resources that relate to goats, including the Charlie And Isabella's Magical Adventures Series of Children's Books, suitable for bed-time reading that are beautifully illustrated.

Goat Knowledge Series Titles

How To Keep Goats Healthy #1
ISBN: 978-1-78165-021-9

Golden Guernsey Goats #2
ISBN: 978-1-78165-022-6

A Simple Guide To The Goat's
Digestive System #3
ISBN: 978-1-78165-024-0

Success Guide For Raising
Healthy Goats #4
ISBN: 978-1-78165-026-4

Managing Goat Nutrition: What
You Need To Know A Simple

Guide   #5

ISBN: 978-1-78165-027-1

Plants And Goats An Easy To
Read   Guide   #6

ISBN: 978-1-78165-038-7

Goat Housing, Bedding, Fencing,
Exercise Yards And Pasture
Management   Guide   #7

ISBN: 978-1-78165-040-0

Weaning Your Goat Kids A
Simple   Guide   #8

ISBN: 978-1-78165-042-4

How To Breed Goats And
Manage Gestation A Simple

Guide   #9

ISBN: 978-1-78165-045-5

Milking Your Goats What You
Need To Know Guide #10
ISBN: 978-1-78165-047-9

Water, Vitamins, Minerals And
Dietary Needs For Goats A
Simple   Guide   #11
ISBN: 978-1-78165-049-3

How To Care For Your Newborn
Goat Kids A Simple Guide #12
ISBN: 978-1-78165-051-6

Other Goat Books And Articles

By

Felicity McCullough

www.goatlapshop.com

A Simple Guide To The Goat's Digestive System

Boar Goats

Charlie And Isabella's Magical Adventure

Charlie And Isabella Meet Jacob

Charlie And Isabella's Second Adventure With Jacob

Charlie And Isabella's Magical Adventures Compendium

Diseases of Goats

Goat Basics

Goat Breed: Golden Guernsey Goats

Goat Videos

How To Keep Goats Healthy

Nigerian Dwarf Goats

Nimbkar Boer Goat

Easy Guide To Raising and Caring for Goats

Nimbkar Boer Goat (article)

Schallenberg Virus (article)

Success Guide For Raising Healthy Goats

The Fun of Goats

My Lap Shop Publishers

Plymouth, England

www.mylapshop.com